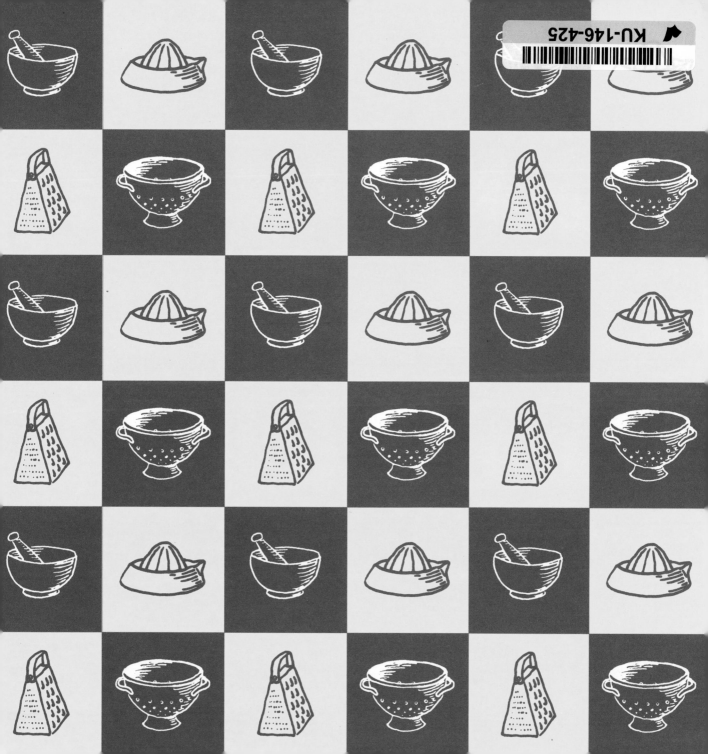

# COFFEE

# COFFEE

*A Book of Recipes*

INTRODUCTION BY CHRIS INGRAM

LORENZ BOOKS

This edition first published in 1998 by Lorenz Books

© Anness Publishing Limited 1998

Lorenz Books is an imprint of
Anness Publishing Limited
Hermes House
88-89 Blackfriars Road
London SE1 8HA

This edition distributed in Canada by Raincoast Books
8680 Cambie Street Vancouver British Columbia V6P 6M9

ISBN 1 85967 550 6

A CIP catalogue record is available from the British Library

*Publisher* Joanna Lorenz
*Senior Cookery Editor* Linda Fraser
*Project Editor* Margaret Malone
*Designer* Bill Mason
*Illustrations* Anna Koska

*Photographers* Karl Adamson, William Adams-Lingwood, Edward Allwright, David Armstrong, Steve Baxter, James Duncan,
Michelle Garrett, Amanda Heywood, David Jordan and Don Last
*Recipes* Angela Boggiano, Carla Capalbo, Jacqueline Clark, Frances Cleary, Carole Clements, Joanna Farrow,
Christine France, Shirley Gill, Carole Handslip, Ruby Le Bois, Norma Miller, Janice Murfitt, Stuart Walton, Laura Washburn,
Kate Whiteman, Elizabeth Wolf-Cohen and Jeni Wright
*Food for photography* Carole Handslip, Jane Hartshorn, Lucy McKelvie, Jane Stevenson, Judy Williams and Elizabeth Wolf-Cohen
*Stylists* Diana Civil, Maria Kelly, Blake Minton and Marian Price
*Jacket photography* Janine Hosegood

For all recipes, quantities are given in both metric and imperial measures and, where appropriate,
measures are also given in standard cups and spoons. Follow one set, but not a mixture,
because they are not interchangeable.

Printed and bound in China

3 5 7 9 10 8 6 4 2

# Contents

# $\mathscr{I}$NTRODUCTION

In the history of food, particularly in the West, coffee is one of the youngsters; it has been known in this part of the world only since the end of the 17th century. Yet, in spite of its relative newness, coffee has become one of our favourite ingredients, loved not only as a beverage but also as an indispensable and delicious flavouring in all sorts of dishes. It is perhaps not surprising that the better-known coffee recipes originate from countries like Italy, France and America where coffee is the most popular non-alcoholic beverage.

There is little evidence to show how coffee was discovered, but it is known that it was enjoyed as a drink for centuries in the Near and Middle East before the Venetians brought it to Europe. Here coffee houses sprang up, frequented by the intelligentsia and the fashionable elite, who would spend hours drinking coffee and talking over issues of the day.

Coffee can be grown only in tropical regions but once Europe acquired a taste for it, plants were taken to South America and the Caribbean and coffee growing quickly became established. These areas, with their slave labour, provided a large and cheap labour force. Today coffee is grown and exported from more than fifty countries.

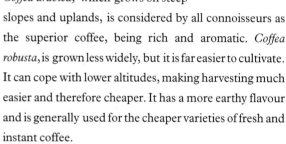

There are essentially only two types of coffee plant of significance. *Coffea arabica,* which grows on steep slopes and uplands, is considered by all connoisseurs as the superior coffee, being rich and aromatic. *Coffea robusta,* is grown less widely, but it is far easier to cultivate. It can cope with lower altitudes, making harvesting much easier and therefore cheaper. It has a more earthy flavour and is generally used for the cheaper varieties of fresh and instant coffee.

After harvesting, the coffee fruit (called the cherry) is left to ripen for six to eight months and the dried skins and pulp are removed. Inside the fruit lie the pale coffee beans, which are sorted and graded and then exported, to be roasted by the country of import.

The characteristics valued in coffee are good acidity (which provides sharpness), body and aroma. Most of the coffee sold today in shops is a number of different coffees, blended in order to combine or neutralize these characteristics. In cooking, the same rich flavour and aroma can transform almost any cake or dessert. This book features many classic coffee dishes, including Tiramisu Tart and Mocha Brazil Layer Torte, plus new combinations such as Coffee Jellies and Iced Coffee and Nut Meringue. All highlight the importance of coffee in providing a flavour ranging from the subtle to the exotic.

# Types of Coffee

### BRAZILIAN

Brazil is the world's largest coffee grower, producing many different grades of coffee, most of which are used for the manufacture of instant coffee. Best of the Brazilian beans is Brazilian Santos, particularly Bourbon Santos.

### COLOMBIAN

Another large exporter of coffee, Colombian beans are medium- or dark-roasted and have a heady aroma. Best-known of the Colombian coffees is Medellin Excelso, which has a mildly acid, slightly nutty flavour.

### COSTA RICAN

Mountain-grown beans are known for their high acidity. However, the majority of beans produced here have a rich, smooth flavour and fragrance. Tarrazu is considered among the best of Costa Rican coffees.

### GUATEMALAN

Beans from the higher areas of Guatemala produce full-flavoured coffee and are known for their high acidity. Other regions produce beans that have a pleasant, but milder, spiciness and consequently medium-roast is recommended.

### INDONESIAN

Best-known of these coffees are those from Java and Sumatra with their smooth flavour.

### JAMAICAN

Most prized of Jamaican coffees is Blue Mountain. Thought by many to be the best coffee in the world, its wonderful aroma and delicate flavour are due to the natural sugars in the bean caramelizing during roasting.

### KENYAN

The Kenyan peaberry produces single round beans and is famed for its good flavour and acidity. It is considered so fine that it is rarely blended and should be drunk black.

### UNROASTED BEANS

Before roasting, the seeds of the different types of coffee plant are fairly similar in colour, varying from yellow to green, and in shape from round to oval. Though it is possible to buy unroasted coffee beans, it is the roasting process that develops coffee's aromatic qualitites.

### CONTINENTAL BLEND/ESPRESSO BLEND

Blends of a variety of dark-roasted coffee beans to give a full-bodied sharp taste and bite.

*Costa Rican light*

*Costa Rican dark*

*Colombian unroasted*

*Brazilian light*

*Honduras dark*

*Colombian medium*

*Kenyan light*

*Espresso blend dark*

*Continental blend high*

## ROASTING

*Light Roast* Suitable for mild coffees with a delicate aroma and flavour that would be lost with stronger roasting. The coffee beans are medium brown in colour.

*Medium Roast* The best roast for coffees with a well-defined character. It gives a stronger flavour yet is still suitable for drinking black or with milk.

*Full or Dark Roast* Full or dark roast gives a strong aroma and a full-bodied, slightly bitter flavour.

*High or Continental Roast* This accentuates the strong, bitter aspects of coffee. The beans are almost black.

## GRINDS

*Coarse Ground* Normally only obtained by grinding at home. Coffee will be lighter and less full-bodied than more finely ground coffee.

*Medium/Medium Fine Ground* Readily available ready-ground, or grind at home. Suitable for fairly light coffees made in cafetière or balloon/vacuum method.

*Espresso Ground* Produces a stronger coffee with a good full-bodied flavour. The finer grind means there is a greater surface area for the water to filter through.

*Very Fine Ground* The best choice for making espresso.

*Pulverized* Also known as powdered coffee (not to be confused with instant coffee), this produces the strongest of coffees. The grinding process generates heat that intensifies the flavour of the coffee beans.

## INSTANT COFFEE

Instant coffee is made from coffee beans that have been brewed into a concentrate.

*Coffee Granules* The best instant coffees use arabica coffee which has been freeze-dried and processed.

*Coffee Powder* Generally cheaper than granules and made from robusta beans. The coffee concentrate is dried to make a fine powder.

*Coffee Bags* These aim to give the convenience of instant coffee with the flavour of brewed coffee but the resulting coffee is disappointing, often lacking any kind of body.

*Instant Espresso* Sold in individual sachets, it is the strongest and most full-bodied of instant coffees.

## COFFEE ESSENCE

Useful for flavouring cakes and desserts. However, be sure to buy pure coffee essence and not chicory and coffee which is still widely available.

## COFFEE LIQUEUR

The best-known coffee liqueur is Tia Maria, a Jamaican rum liqueur made with coffee extracts and spices.

## CHOCOLATE-COVERED COFFEE BEANS

Roasted coffee beans covered in chocolate. Serve with coffee or use as a decoration for cakes and desserts.

## SYRUPS FOR FLAVOURING COFFEE

There are many flavours to choose from, including vanilla, hazelnut and Irish Cream. Add to freshly brewed coffee.

*Coffee bag*

*Turkish pulverized*

*Coffee essence*

*Fine ground dark blend espresso*

*Instant granules*

*Syrup for flavouring coffee*

*Coarse ground light Colombian*

*Instant espresso*

*Chocolate-covered coffee beans*

*Coffee liqueur*

# $\mathcal{B}$ASIC $\mathcal{T}$ECHNIQUES

## USING FRESH COFFEE

It is important to choose the correct grind of coffee to suit the method of brewing. The finer the grain, the greater the surface area that is exposed to the water and the slower the water will run through it. Consequently coffee will be more full-bodied and stronger.

Coffee machines are designed for a particular grind of coffee and if this is not right the resulting coffee will be either weak and thin-tasting, if the grains are too coarse, or bitter and harsh if the grind is too fine.

If buying a coffee grinder, choose one that can be adjusted according to the grind required. If your present coffee grinder can't be adjusted, learn to judge the fineness of the grind. Coarse-ground should be the consistency of granulated sugar, pulverized to the consistency of icing sugar, with the others coming on a scale in between.

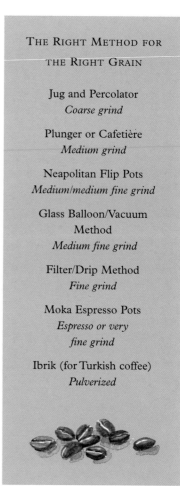

THE RIGHT METHOD FOR
THE RIGHT GRAIN

**Jug and Percolator**
*Coarse grind*

**Plunger or Cafetière**
*Medium grind*

**Neapolitan Flip Pots**
*Medium/medium fine grind*

**Glass Balloon/Vacuum Method**
*Medium fine grind*

**Filter/Drip Method**
*Fine grind*

**Moka Espresso Pots**
*Espresso or very fine grind*

**Ibrik (for Turkish coffee)**
*Pulverized*

*Choose a grinder that allows you to control the degree of grind and ensures an even grind every time.*

*A refinement of the old-fashioned jug method. Use only coarse or medium grinds or the coffee will be cloudy.*

## BUYING COFFEE

For best flavour, buy coffee beans from a good coffee shop. They will be freshly roasted and should be used within a week. Freshly roasted beans can be frozen for up to 6 months, with little or no loss of flavour. If purchasing from supermarkets, buy the vacuum-packed coffees, which will last, unopened, until the use-by date on the packet. Once opened, however, all coffee, and ground coffee particularly, will lose its flavour quickly. Consequently, buy only small quantities of coffee beans and grind just prior to use. Coffee beans and ground coffee should be stored in an airtight container in the fridge. The exception are espresso blends: the dark-roasted beans react adversely to chilling, as the oil in the beans tends to coagulate.

### DECAFFEINATED COFFEE

*Caffeine is present in all coffee and is a known stimulant, affecting the central nervous system and stimulating the action of the heart and lungs. Although enjoyed by many for this very reason, others react badly to it. To remove the caffeine, coffee beans are soaked in water or treated with solvents or carbon dioxide. This last method is considered the best as it does not affect the flavour and there is no residue.*

*Decaffeinated coffee contains less than 0.9 per cent caffeine, so that a small cup of coffee contains 3mg of caffeine, compared to about 115mg for filter coffee and 65mg for instant coffee. Decaffeinated ground or whole beans, as well as instant coffee, are available from almost all supermarkets.*

### COFFEE-BREWING TIPS

- Use fresh, cold water.
- Never use boiling water: water should be just off the boil, at 92–96°C/198–205°F.
- Drink as soon as possible after brewing.
- Always keep coffee equipment scrupulously clean.
- The quantity of coffee required for brewed coffee will depend partly on the brewing method and partly on taste. As a rule, however, use 25–30ml/1½–2 tbsp ground coffee per cup.

- For Turkish coffee, 1 heaped teaspoon each of coffee and sugar per cup will make a strong coffee.
- In recipes calling for brewed coffee, make up according to your preferred method, or reserve a little coffee from breakfast or lunch. Since coffee will be blended with other ingredients and will frequently be reheated in the recipe, the coffee does not have to be freshly made.

## COFFEE MAKERS

*Coffee Jug:* This is the simplest of all methods, although not the preferred among the cognoscenti. Coffee is brewed like tea, with water circulating around the coffee grains. Use about 65–75ml/4$\frac{1}{2}$–5 tbsp coffee to 600ml/1 pint/2$\frac{1}{2}$ cups water. Warm the pot before adding coarse-ground coffee. Stir the mixture after adding hot water and leave to stand for about 4 minutes before serving. Use a strainer when pouring.

*Cafetière:* This is a sophisticated version of the jug method. Nearly boiling water is poured over the coffee and is allowed to infuse for 3–4 minutes. The plunger is then pushed down, forcing the grains to the bottom of the cafetière so that the liquid can be poured. Use 65–75ml/4$\frac{1}{2}$–5 tbsp medium-ground coffee to 600ml/1 pint/2$\frac{1}{2}$ cups water and stir thoroughly before allowing to stand.

*Filter Maker:* This is probably the most popular method and produces a fine, relatively strong coffee. Fine-ground coffee is spooned into a filter paper in a holder over a pot and nearly boiling water is poured over. The coffee gradually drips through to the pot, which should be kept warm over a low heat. Use the same quantity of coffee as for the jug method.

*Filter Machine:* This is simply an automatic version of the filter maker. Follow the manufacturer's instructions and aim to keep the coffee in the jug for no more than $\frac{1}{2}$ hour. Use 75ml/5 tbsp coffee to 600ml/1 pint/2$\frac{1}{2}$ cups water.

*Percolator:* Medium-ground coffee is placed in a basket and boiling water, heated in the machine, is forced through the coffee. The disadvantage of this method is that the same boiling water circulates continuously. Although once very popular, the percolator is rather disdained by coffee experts. Use the same quantity of coffee as for the jug method.

*Espresso Machine:* Espresso coffee can be made using a moka pot or by machine, both working on the same principle of forcing steam and water through very fine, dark-roasted coffee grounds. Pour the coffee as soon as it has 'gurgled' through, otherwise it may burn. If using a moka machine, always fill the coffee basket to the top with ground coffee.

## CLASSIC COFFEE DRINKS

### MOCHA ON A CLOUD

Blend 600ml/1 pint/2½ cups strong brewed coffee with 475ml/16fl oz/2 cups hot milk in a jug and keep warm. Bring to the boil a further 750ml/1¼ pints/3 cups milk with 45ml/3 tbsp vanilla sugar and 2–3 drops vanilla essence. Reduce the heat, add 115g/4oz plain chocolate broken into squares and heat gently, whisking until melted. Pour the chocolate milk into the jug and whisk until frothy. Serve in tall mugs or glasses, topped with cream, a cinnamon stick and a sprinkling of nutmeg.

### SOUTHERN ICED COFFEE

A delicious variation of iced coffee. Infuse 4 cinnamon sticks and 6 cloves with 1 litre/1¾ pints/4 cups freshly made strong black coffee, adding 45–60ml/3–4 tbsp sugar to taste.

Leave for about 1 hour, then strain the coffee into a large jug and add 60ml/4 tbsp Tia Maria or other coffee liqueur. Add plenty of ice cubes and pour into chilled glasses.

### CAFE BRULOT

Brew 475ml/16fl oz/2 cups strong coffee, using the filter method, and keep warm. Carefully pare the rind of 1 orange and 1 lemon, preferably in one long strip. Place the rinds in a small pan and add 4 sugar lumps, 6 cloves, 1 cinnamon stick, 175ml/6fl oz/¾ cup brandy and 45–60ml/3–4 tbsp curaçao or orange liqueur. Heat very gently until the sugar lumps dissolve, stirring continuously. When the liquid is very hot, ignite it, then slowly add the coffee in a thin stream. Pour into glasses and serve at once with a cinnamon stick and orange rind garnish.

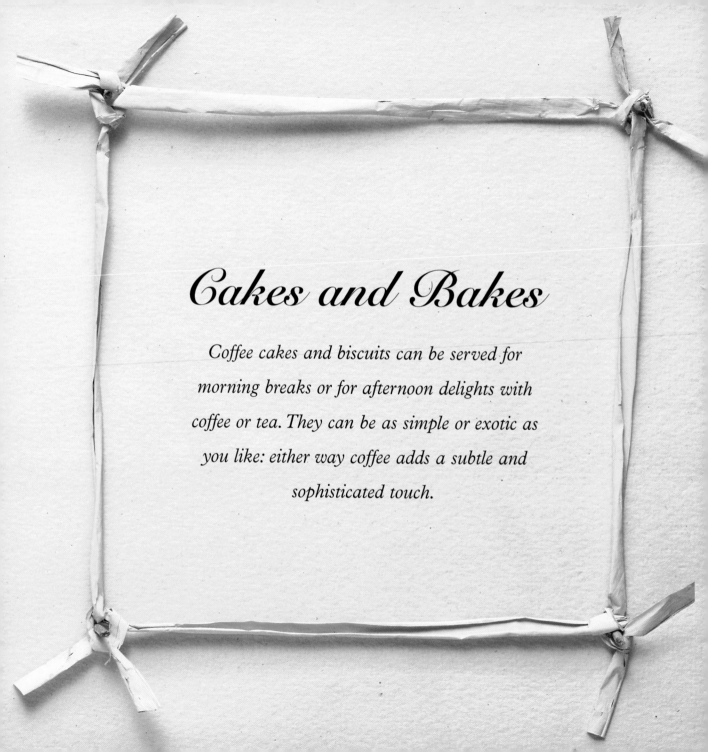

# Cakes and Bakes

*Coffee cakes and biscuits can be served for morning breaks or for afternoon delights with coffee or tea. They can be as simple or exotic as you like: either way coffee adds a subtle and sophisticated touch.*

# COFFEE SPONGE DROPS

*The coffee-flavoured sponge in these soft cakes contrasts beautifully with the ginger filling. If using coffee granules, crush them so that they can be sifted with the flour.*

**Makes 12**

*50g/2oz/¹/₂ cup plain flour*

*15ml/1 tbsp instant coffee granules, crushed, or coffee powder*

*2 eggs*

*75g/3oz/6 tbsp caster sugar*

**For the filling**

*115g/4oz/¹/₂ cup low-fat soft cheese*

*40g/1¹/₂ oz/¹/₄ cup stem ginger, chopped*

**COOK'S TIP**

*Always work quickly and lightly when making sponge cakes. Sift the flour and coffee and whisk the eggs and sugar in order to incorporate as much air as possible. The two should be folded together carefully using a metal spoon to avoid knocking out any air.*

Make the filling by beating together the soft cheese and stem ginger and chill until required. Preheat the oven to 190°C/375°F/Gas 5 and line two baking sheets with non-stick baking paper.

Sift the flour and coffee together in a bowl and whisk the eggs and caster sugar together in a separate bowl until thick and creamy. Add the sifted flour and coffee and fold in with a metal spoon.

Spoon the mixture into a piping bag fitted with a 1cm/¹/₂in plain nozzle and pipe 4cm/1¹/₂in rounds on to the baking sheets. Bake in the oven for 12 minutes, then cool on a wire rack. Sandwich together with the filling.

# MISSISSIPPI COFFEE CAKE

*This dense, moist American cake has a rich coffee flavour and is utterly delicious.*

**Serves 8–10**

*225g/8oz/2 cups plain flour*

*5ml/1 tsp baking powder*

*300ml/½ pint/1¼ cups hot, strong
    brewed coffee*

*50ml/2fl oz/¼ cup brandy*

*150g/5oz unsweetened chocolate,
    in squares*

*225g/8oz/1 cup butter, diced*

*225g/8oz/generous 1 cup caster sugar*

*2 eggs, lightly beaten*

*7.5ml/1½ tsp vanilla essence*

*pinch of salt*

*cocoa powder, for dusting*

*whipped cream or ice cream, to serve*

COOK'S TIP

*Unsweetened chocolate is available
in specialist shops. However, if
you can't find any, use a plain
chocolate or use 150g/5oz/
1¼ cups cocoa powder and an
extra 50g/2oz/4 tbsp butter.*

Preheat the oven to 140°C/275°F/Gas 1. Grease a large fluted ring mould and dust with cocoa powder.

Sift the flour, baking powder and salt into a bowl. Place the coffee, brandy, chocolate and butter in a heatproof bowl over a pan of simmering water and heat until the chocolate and butter have melted, stirring occasionally. Pour the melted mixture into a mixing bowl and carefully whisk in the sugar by hand, continuing to whisk until all the sugar has dissolved. Whisk in the flour mixture and then gradually whisk in the eggs and the vanilla essence, until the mixture is smooth.

Pour the mixture into the prepared tin and bake in the oven for about 1 hour 20 minutes or until a skewer inserted into the cake comes out clean. Cool the cake in the tin for 15 minutes and then unmould on to a wire rack. Cool completely and then dust lightly with cocoa powder. Serve with whipped cream or ice cream.

# MOCHA VIENNESE SWIRLS

*No one will be able to resist these delightful, melt-in-the-mouth marvels. With their coffee-chocolate flavour they are an excellent choice for a sophisticated tea party. Make lots, as they will vanish in minutes.*

**Makes about 20**

*115g/4oz plain chocolate, broken*
   *into squares*
*200g/7oz/scant 1 cup unsalted*
   *butter, softened*
*50g/2oz/¹/₂ cup icing sugar*
*30ml/2 tbsp strong brewed coffee*
*200g/7oz/1³/₄ cups plain flour*
*50g/2oz/¹/₂ cup cornflour*

**For the decoration**
*about 20 blanched almonds*
*150g/5oz plain chocolate*

Preheat the oven to 190°C/375°F/Gas 5 and lightly grease two large baking sheets. Melt the chocolate in a bowl over a pan of simmering water and cream the butter with the icing sugar in a bowl until smooth and pale. Beat in the melted chocolate and then stir in the coffee.

Sift the flour and cornflour into the mixture and fold in with a metal spoon. Spoon the mixture into a piping bag fitted with a star nozzle and pipe about 20 well-spaced swirls on to the baking sheets.

Press an almond into the centre of each swirl and bake for about 15 minutes or until the biscuits are firm and lightly golden. Cool for 10 minutes on the baking sheets, then transfer to a wire rack to cool completely. Melt the chocolate and dip in each biscuit to coat the base. Leave to set on a sheet of non-stick baking paper.

**COOK'S TIP**

*If the mixture is too stiff to pipe easily, soften it with a little more black coffee.*

# CAPPUCCINO COFFEE CAKE

*This moist cake really does have the flavour of cappuccino. Serve it with coffee for an afternoon treat.*

**Serves 8–10**

*15ml/1 tbsp instant coffee granules*

*175g/6oz plain chocolate*

*5 eggs, separated*

*150g/5oz/³/4 cup sugar*

*chocolate-covered coffee beans,*
*    to decorate*

**For the coffee cream filling**

*175ml/6fl oz/³/4 cup whipping or*
*    double cream*

*25g/1oz/2 tbsp sugar*

*225g/8oz/1 cup mascarpone or*
*    cream cheese, softened*

*30ml/2 tbsp Tia Maria*

*25g/1oz plain chocolate, grated*

**For the coffee buttercream**

*4 egg yolks*

*60ml/4 tbsp golden syrup*

*50g/2oz/¹/4 cup sugar*

*225g/8oz/1 cup unsalted butter*

*30ml/2 tbsp instant coffee granules*

*15–30ml/1–2 tbsp Tia Maria*

Preheat the oven to 180°C/350°F/Gas 4 and line a 37 x 25cm/15 x 10in baking sheet with non-stick baking paper. Dissolve the coffee in 45ml/ 3 tbsp hot water. In a bowl over a pan of simmering water heat the chocolate and dissolved coffee until melted and smooth. Whisk the egg yolks and sugar until thick and pale, and add the chocolate mixture, whisking well.

Whisk the egg whites until fairly stiff and fold into the chocolate mixture. Pour the mixture into the prepared tin and bake for 12–15 minutes until firm. Turn the cake out on to a wire rack, peel off the paper and cool.

Make the filling: whip the cream and sugar. Beat the mascarpone or cream cheese and liqueur in a separate bowl and stir in the grated chocolate. Fold into the whipped cream and chill until ready to use.

Make the buttercream: beat the egg yolks until thickened. Heat the syrup and sugar until the mixture boils, stirring constantly. Slowly pour the hot syrup over the egg yolks in a steady stream, beating all the time, until the mixture feels cool, then gradually add the butter in small pieces, beating until smooth. Dissolve the coffee in 15–25ml/1–1¹/2 tbsp hot water and add to the mixture along with the liqueur.

Slice the cake crossways into three and spread two strips with the coffee cream filling. Assemble the cake and spread with some of the buttercream. Pipe the remaining buttercream in a lattice pattern over the cake and decorate with chocolate-covered coffee beans.

# COFFEE, PEACH AND ALMOND DAQUOISE

*This is a traditional meringue gâteau, filled with a rich coffee buttercream and layered with peaches.*

**Serves 12**

*5 egg whites*

*275g/10oz/1¼ cups caster sugar*

*15g/½oz/2 tbsp cornflour*

*175g/6oz/1½ cups ground almonds,*
  *toasted*

**For the custard**

*5 egg yolks*

*150g/5oz/¾ cup caster sugar*

*125ml/4½ fl oz/generous ½ cup milk*

*275g/10oz/1¼ cups unsalted butter,*
  *diced*

*45–60ml/3–4 tbsp coffee essence*

*2 × 400g/14oz cans peach halves,*
  *drained and chopped, 3 halves*
  *reserved for decoration*

*icing sugar, for dusting*

*toasted flaked almonds and a few*
  *mint leaves, to decorate*

Preheat the oven to 150°C/300°F/Gas 2 and draw three 23cm/9in circles on to three sheets of non-stick baking paper. Place each on a separate baking sheet. Whisk the egg whites until stiff and gradually add the sugar, whisking until the mixture is thick and glossy. Fold in the cornflour and ground almonds. Spoon the mixture into a piping bag fitted with a plain nozzle and pipe in a continuous tight coil on to each prepared piece of baking paper, starting at the centre and gradually filling the circle. Bake for 1¾–2 hours until lightly golden and dried out. Peel away the paper and cool on a wire rack.

Make the custard: whisk the egg yolks with the sugar until thick and pale. Heat the milk in a pan until nearly boiling and pour over the egg mixture. Return the mixture to the pan and cook gently until just thickened. Cool slightly and strain into a bowl. Beat in the butter a little at a time until thickened and stir in the coffee essence.

Trim the meringue neatly, crushing any trimmings. Fold the chopped peaches and meringue trimmings into half of the custard and use this to sandwich the meringue circles together. Coat the top and sides of the meringue with the remaining custard and decorate with toasted almond flakes. Dust with icing sugar and finish with fans of the reserved peaches and a few mint leaves.

# TIA MARIA GATEAU

*This feather-light coffee sponge has a creamy filling, flavoured with delicious Tia Maria coffee liqueur.*

**Serves 8**

*75g/3oz/³⁄₄ cup plain flour*
*30ml/2 tbsp instant coffee powder*
*3 eggs*
*115g/4oz/¹⁄₂ cup caster sugar*
*coffee beans, to decorate*

**For the filling**

*175g/6oz/³⁄₄ cup low-fat soft cheese*
*15ml/1 tbsp clear honey*
*15ml/1 tbsp Tia Maria or other*
  *coffee liqueur*
*40g/1¹⁄₂oz/¹⁄₄ cup stem ginger,*
  *roughly chopped*

**For the icing**

*225g/8oz/2 cups icing sugar*
*10ml/2 tsp coffee essence or instant*
  *coffee dissolved in 10ml/2 tsp*
  *hot water*
*5ml/1 tsp cocoa powder*

Preheat the oven to 190°C/375°F/Gas 5. Grease and line a deep 20cm/8in round cake tin. Sift together the flour and coffee powder. Place the eggs and caster sugar in a bowl and whisk until thick and pale. Fold in the flour mixture with a metal spoon, being careful not to knock out any air. Spoon into the prepared tin. Bake for 30–35 minutes until the cake is firm. Remove from the tin and cool on a wire rack.

Make the filling: blend the cheese with the honey, beating until smooth. Stir in the coffee liqueur and chopped ginger. Split the cake in half horizontally and sandwich the two halves together with the filling.

For the icing, mix the icing sugar and coffee with enough water to make an icing that will coat the back of a wooden spoon. Spread three-quarters of the icing over the cake smoothing it evenly to the edges. Stir the cocoa into the remaining icing and pipe this mocha icing over the top. Decorate with coffee beans.

# WALNUT COFFEE TORTE

*Walnuts and coffee are perfect partners in this sumptuous confection, coated with chocolate frosting.*

**Serves 8–10**

*150g/5oz/1¼ cups walnuts*

*150g/5oz/¾ cup caster sugar*

*5 eggs, separated*

*20g/¾ oz/4 tbsp dried breadcrumbs*

*15ml/1 tbsp cocoa powder*

*15ml/1 tbsp instant coffee granules*
*or powder*

*30ml/2 tbsp rum or lemon juice*

*90ml/6 tbsp redcurrant jelly*

*chopped walnuts, to decorate*

**For the frosting**

*225g/8oz plain chocolate*

*750ml/1¼ pints/3 cups whipping*
*cream*

---

**COOK'S TIP**

*If desired, make a starburst pattern in the frosting by pressing gently with a table knife in lines radiating out from the centre.*

---

First make the frosting: break the chocolate into a large bowl, add the cream and place over a pan of simmering water. Heat gently, stirring, until the chocolate melts. Allow to cool, then cover and place in the fridge until the mixture is firm.

Preheat the oven to 180°C/350°F/Gas 4 and line a 23cm/9in round cake tin with non-stick baking paper. Place the nuts and 45ml/3 tbsp of the sugar in a food processor and blend until the nuts are finely chopped. Whisk together the egg yolks and remaining sugar until thick and pale. Fold in the walnuts and then stir in the breadcrumbs, cocoa, coffee and rum or lemon juice.

In a separate bowl, whisk the egg whites until stiff. Fold into the walnut mixture and pour into the prepared tin. Bake for about 45 minutes until the top of the cake is firm and springy. Stand for 5 minutes and transfer to a rack.

When the cake is cool, slice horizontally. Beat the chocolate frosting with an electric mixer until fairly soft but not grainy. Melt the jelly in a saucepan and brush a little over one cake layer. Spread with some of the chocolate frosting and sandwich with the second layer of cake. Brush the top of the cake with the remaining jelly and then cover the sides and top with the remaining chocolate frosting. Sprinkle the chopped walnuts around the edge.

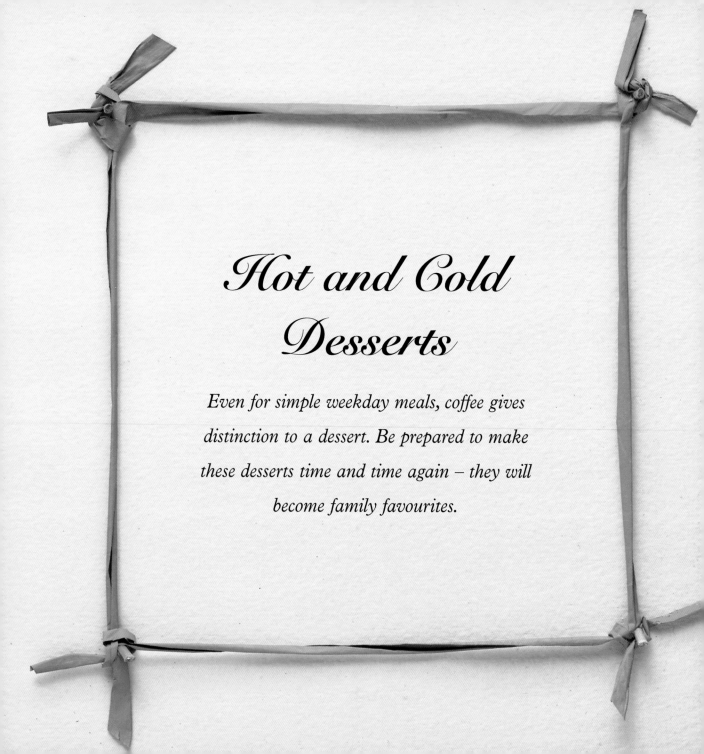

# Hot and Cold Desserts

*Even for simple weekday meals, coffee gives distinction to a dessert. Be prepared to make these desserts time and time again – they will become family favourites.*

# CHOCOLATE AND COFFEE PUDDING

*A dream of a pudding that makes its own heavenly coffee-chocolate sauce as it cooks.*

### Serves 4–6

75g/3oz/³/4 cup plain flour

10ml/2 tsp baking powder

25g/1oz plain chocolate, broken
    into pieces

50g/2oz/4 tbsp butter

115g/4oz/¹/2 cup caster sugar

100ml/3fl oz/¹/3 cup milk

1.5ml/¹/4 tsp vanilla essence

pinch of salt

whipped cream, to serve

### For the topping

90g/3¹/2oz/¹/2 cup dark brown sugar

65g/2¹/2oz/¹/4 cup caster sugar

30ml/2 tbsp cocoa powder

30ml/2 tbsp instant coffee granules
    or powder dissolved in 300ml/
    ¹/2 pint/1¹/4 cups hot water, cooled

Preheat the oven to 180°C/350°F/Gas 4 and grease a 23cm/9in square non-stick baking tin. For the topping, mix together the two sugars and stir in the cocoa. Set aside.

Sift the flour, baking powder and salt into a bowl. Place the chocolate, butter and caster sugar in a large bowl and set over a pan of simmering water. Heat gently, stirring occasionally, until the chocolate and butter have melted. Remove the bowl from the heat, add the flour mixture and stir well. Stir in the milk and vanilla essence.

Pour the mixture into the prepared tin and sprinkle over the topping mixture. Pour the coffee over the surface and bake in the oven for 40 minutes until firm. Serve hot with whipped cream.

31

# MOCHA RUM SOUFFLES

*The exquisite combination of coffee and chocolate can be fully appreciated in these hot soufflés. Serve them as soon as they are cooked for a fantastic finale to a dinner party.*

**Serves 6**

*30ml/2 tbsp melted unsalted butter*

*65g/2¹/₂oz/generous ¹/₂ cup cocoa powder*

*75g/3oz/¹/₃ cup caster sugar*

*60ml/4 tbsp strong brewed coffee*

*30ml/2 tbsp dark rum*

*6 egg whites*

*icing sugar, for dusting*

Preheat the oven to 190°C/375°F/Gas 5 and place a baking sheet in the oven to preheat. Grease six 250ml/8fl oz/1 cup soufflé dishes with the melted butter. Mix 15ml/1 tbsp of the cocoa powder with 15ml/1 tbsp of the caster sugar in a bowl and tip the mixture into each of the dishes, rotating them to coat evenly. Blend the remaining cocoa with the coffee and rum in a large bowl.

Whisk the egg whites in a separate bowl until stiff peaks form and then whisk in the remaining caster sugar. Stir a generous spoonful of the whites into the cocoa mixture to lighten it and then fold in the remaining whites. Spoon the mixture into the prepared dishes. Place the soufflé dishes on the baking sheet (this will help the soufflés cook through), and bake for 12–15 minutes until well risen. Serve at once, dusted with icing sugar.

COOK'S TIP

*When serving the soufflés at the end of a dinner party, prepare them just before the meal is served. Pop in the oven as soon as the main course is finished and serve freshly baked.*

# COFFEE JELLIES

*These jellies should have a strong and distinct coffee flavour and are best made using a high-roasted arabica bean. They are served with an unusual textured amaretti cream.*

**Serves 4**

*75g/3oz/6 tbsp caster sugar*

*450ml/¾ pint/2 cups hot strong brewed coffee*

*30–45ml/2–3 tbsp Tia Maria or other coffee liqueur*

*20ml/4 tsp powdered gelatine*

**For the coffee amaretti cream**

*150ml/¼ pint/⅔ cup double or whipping cream*

*15ml/1 tbsp icing sugar, sifted*

*10–15ml/2–3 tsp instant coffee granules or powder, dissolved in 15ml/1 tbsp hot water*

*6 large amaretti biscuits, crushed, 30ml/2 tbsp of the crumbs reserved to decorate*

---

COOK'S TIP

*To ensure that the jellies are crystal clear, filter the coffee through a paper filter.*

---

Place the sugar in a pan with 75ml/5 tbsp water and stir over a gentle heat until dissolved. Increase the heat and boil the syrup steadily, without stirring, for 3–4 minutes. Stir the hot coffee and liqueur into the syrup. Sprinkle the gelatine over the top, stirring until it is completely dissolved. Pour the mixture into four wetted individual moulds, cool and then chill in the fridge for several hours until set.

Make the amaretti cream: lightly whip the cream with the icing sugar until it holds stiff peaks. Stir in the coffee and then gently fold in all but 30ml/2 tbsp of the crushed biscuits. Unmould the jellies on to individual serving plates and spoon a little of the coffee amaretti cream to one side. Dust over the reserved amaretti crumbs and serve at once.

# COFFEE AND MACADAMIA CREAMS

*The intense flavour of the coffee liqueur is perfectly complemented by melt-in-the-mouth meringue biscuits.*

**Serves 4–6**

*10ml/2 tsp powdered gelatine*

*350ml/12fl oz/1½ cups double*
*cream*

*150ml/¼ pint/⅔ cup thick natural*
*yogurt*

*15ml/1 tbsp strong brewed coffee*

*25g/1oz/¼ cup icing sugar*

*15ml/1 tbsp Kahlúa or other*
*coffee liqueur*

*50g/2oz/½ cup macadamia nuts,*
*toasted and chopped*

*toasted macadamia nuts and*
*chocolate coffee beans, to decorate*

**For the meringue finger biscuits**

*1 egg white*

*50g/2oz/¼ cup caster sugar*

Make the meringue fingers: preheat the oven to 120°C/250°F/Gas ½ and line a baking sheet with non-stick baking paper. Whisk the egg white until stiff, whisk in half the sugar and then fold in the rest. Pipe finger shapes of meringue on to the baking sheet and bake for 2½ hours.

Meanwhile, make the creams: sprinkle the gelatine over 45ml/3 tbsp water in a small heatproof bowl. Set over a pan of simmering water and stir until dissolved. Blend the cream, yogurt, coffee, icing sugar and liqueur in a bowl. Stir in the dissolved gelatine and chill until just setting. Stir in the nuts and spoon into small moulds. Chill until firm, then unmould and decorate with nuts and beans. Serve with the meringue fingers.

# BRAZILIAN COFFEE BANANAS

*Rich and lavish-looking, this low-calorie dessert, combining coffee with bananas, has a heavenly flavour and takes only about 2 minutes to make!*

**Serves 4**

4 small ripe bananas

15ml/1 tbsp lemon juice

15ml/1 tbsp instant coffee granules or
  powder dissolved in 15ml/1 tbsp
  hot water, cooled

30ml/2 tbsp muscovado sugar

250ml/8fl oz/1 cup Greek yogurt

15ml/1 tbsp flaked almonds, toasted

COOK'S TIP

*For a special occasion, add a
dash of dark rum or brandy to
the mashed bananas for extra
richness.*

Peel and slice 1 banana, sprinkle with the lemon juice and set aside for decoration. Mash the remaining 3 bananas and stir in the coffee. Divide half of the mixture between four serving dishes and sprinkle with sugar. Top with a spoonful of yogurt, make a further layer with the remaining banana mixture and sugar, and end with a swirl of yogurt.

Sprinkle with toasted flaked almonds and decorate with the reserved slices of banana.

# COFFEE-VANILLA-CHOCOLATE CUPS

*This delicious dessert, with layers of coffee, chocolate and vanilla, can be made in advance and is therefore a great choice for dinner parties.*

**Serves 6**

*275g/10oz/1½ cups caster sugar*

*90ml/6 tbsp cornflour*

*about 1 litre/1¾ pints/4 cups milk*

*3 egg yolks*

*75g/3oz/6 tbsp unsalted butter,*
*    softened*

*generous 15ml/1 tbsp instant coffee*
*    granules or powder*

*10ml/2 tsp vanilla essence*

*30ml/2 tbsp cocoa powder*

*whipped cream, to decorate*

COOK'S TIP

*For a special occasion, prepare the vanilla layer using a fresh vanilla pod. Split it down the centre and add to the mixture with the milk. Discard the pod before spooning into the glasses.*

For the coffee layer, mix 90g/3½oz/½ cup of the sugar with 30ml/2 tbsp of the cornflour in a saucepan and blend in 350ml/12fl oz/1¼ cups of the milk. Whisk in 1 egg yolk and then slowly bring to the boil, whisking all the time. Boil for 1 minute until the mixture has thickened and is creamy, continuing to whisk constantly. Remove from the heat and stir in 25g/1oz/2 tbsp of the butter and the coffee granules or powder. Cool slightly and divide among six wine glasses, smoothing the top.

For the vanilla layer, mix a further 90g/3½oz/½ cup of the sugar with 30ml/2 tbsp of the cornflour in a pan and blend in 300ml/½ pint/1¼ cups of the milk. Whisk in 1 egg yolk, bring to the boil and then cook for 1 minute until the mixture has thickened, continuing to whisk constantly. Remove from the heat, add 25g/1oz/2 tbsp of the butter and the vanilla essence. Cool slightly and spoon over the coffee layer.

For the chocolate layer, combine the remaining sugar and cornflour in a pan, blend in the remaining milk and whisk in the last egg yolk. Bring to the boil and cook for 1 minute until the mixture has thickened, continuing to whisk constantly. Remove from the heat and add the remaining butter and the cocoa powder. Cool slightly and spoon over the vanilla layer. Chill until set.

Pipe or spoon a little whipped cream on top of each glass before serving.

# TIRAMISU TART

*Here's an unusual variation on tiramisu made up in three distinct but equally delicious layers.*

### Serves 12–14

*115g/4oz/8 tbsp unsalted butter*

*15ml/1 tbsp coffee liqueur*

*1.5ml/¼ tsp vanilla essence*

*200g/7oz/1¾ cups plain flour*

*25g/1oz/¼ cup cocoa powder*

*25g/1oz/¼ cup icing sugar*

*pinch of salt*

*cocoa powder, for dusting*

### For the chocolate cream

*120ml/4fl oz/½ cup double cream*

*15ml/1 tbsp golden syrup*

*115g/4oz plain chocolate, chopped*

*25g/1oz/2 tbsp unsalted butter, diced*

*30ml/2 tbsp coffee liqueur*

### For the filling

*250ml/8fl oz/1 cup whipping cream*

*350g/12oz/1½ cups mascarpone
    cheese, at room temperature*

*45ml/3 tbsp icing sugar*

*45ml/3 tbsp cold strong brewed coffee*

*45ml/3 tbsp coffee liqueur*

*90g/3½oz plain chocolate, grated*

Make the pastry: melt the butter with the liqueur in a large pan. Remove from the heat and stir in the vanilla essence. Sift together the flour, cocoa, sugar and salt and stir into the butter mixture to make a soft dough. Knead lightly and press into a greased 23cm/9in springform tin. Prick the dough and chill for 40 minutes. Preheat the oven to 190°C/375°F/Gas 5 and bake for 8–10 minutes until firm. If the pastry puffs up, prick with a fork and bake for 2–3 minutes more until set. Cool in the tin.

Meanwhile, make the chocolate cream: heat the cream and syrup until simmering. Remove from the heat and add the chocolate, stirring until melted. Beat the butter pieces into the chocolate mixture together with the liqueur. Pour into the pastry case, cool and then chill in the fridge.

Lastly, make the filling: lightly whip the cream to soft peaks. In another bowl, beat the mascarpone until soft and then beat in the sugar. Add the coffee and liqueur and gently fold in the whipped cream and chocolate. Spoon into the pastry case and chill until ready to serve.

To serve, run a sharp knife around the side of the tin, unclip the tin side and ease the tart out on to a serving plate. Sift a little cocoa over the tart and serve.

# CAPPUCCINO COFFEE CUPS

*Here's the ideal dessert for cappuccino lovers. The same rich, creamy taste, the same wonderful coffee aroma, but made with eggs and crème fraîche for a perfect dessert.*

**Serves 4**

2 eggs

200ml/7fl oz/⁷⁄₈ cup evaporated
   milk, preferably semi-skimmed

25ml/5 tsp instant coffee granules
   or powder

30ml/2 tbsp caster sugar

10ml/2 tsp powdered gelatine

60ml/4 tbsp half-fat crème fraîche

cocoa powder or drinking chocolate
   powder, to serve

eserve one egg white and whisk together the yolk and other egg with the evaporated milk, coffee and sugar in a small pan. Heat very gently until the mixture is hot but not boiling. Continue cooking, stirring all the time, until the mixture is smooth and slightly thickened. Remove the pan from the heat and sprinkle over the gelatine, stirring until it has completely dissolved.

Spoon the coffee custard into four individual dishes and chill until set. Whisk the reserved egg white until stiff and then whisk in the crème fraîche. Spoon the mixture over the desserts. Sprinkle with cocoa or drinking chocolate powder and serve.

**COOK'S TIP**

*For a healthier alternative, Greek yogurt can be used instead of crème fraîche.*

# VELVET MOCHA CREAM PIE

*This American-style pie has an unusual chocolate wafer base and a creamy filling flavoured with*
*chocolate and coffee. Chocolate wafers may be difficult to find, in which case use chocolate-chip cookies.*

Serves 8

**For the base**

*75g/3oz/1½ cups chocolate wafers,*
  *crushed*
*25g/1oz/2 tbsp caster sugar*
*65g/2½oz/5 tbsp butter, melted*

**For the filling**

*175g/6oz plain chocolate*
*25g/1oz unsweetened chocolate*
*350ml/12fl oz/1½ cups whipping*
  *cream*
*15ml/1 tbsp instant coffee granules or*
  *powder dissolved in 30ml/2 tbsp*
  *hot water, cooled*
*whipped cream and chocolate-*
  *covered coffee beans, to decorate*

Make the base: mix together the crushed chocolate wafers and the sugar and stir in the melted butter. Press the mixture evenly over the bottom and sides of a 23cm/9in flan dish and chill in the fridge until firm.

Meanwhile, make the filling: melt the two chocolates in a bowl over a pan of simmering water. Remove from the heat and cool. Whip the cream to soft peaks, add the coffee and continue beating until it just holds its shape. Fold in the chocolate and stir to mix using a metal spoon. Pour into the prepared case and chill until firm. Before serving pipe whipped cream around the edge of the tart and decorate with chocolate-covered coffee beans.

# COFFEE GRANITA

*Granitas are like semi-frozen sorbets and are often served in Italian cafés. Coffee granita is probably the most popular and is very refreshing, particularly in the summer.*

**Serves 6–8**

*30ml/2 tbsp sugar*

*350ml/12fl oz/1½ cups hot strong brewed coffee, preferably espresso*

*250ml/8fl oz/1 cup double cream*

*10ml/2 tsp caster sugar*

Stir the sugar into the hot coffee until dissolved. Leave to cool, pour into a shallow freezer container, cover and freeze for about 1 hour.

When an ice crust has formed around the rim of the container, scrape it away and stir back into the unfrozen coffee. Repeat this process every 30 minutes. After about 2½ hours, the mixture should consist of small, fairly uniform ice crystals and the granita will be ready. Whip the cream with the sugar until stiff. Serve the granita in glasses, each topped with some cream.

# IRISH COFFEE

*Invented at Shannon airport to welcome passengers in the cold winter months, this classic Irish beverage is really a dessert in its own right. As the Irish say, "There's eating and drinking in it!"*

**Makes 4**

*20ml/4 tsp sugar*

*2½ cups strong hot coffee*

*60ml/4 tbsp Irish whiskey*

*250ml/10fl oz/1¼ cups thick heavy cream*

Divide the sugar among four stemmed, heatproof glasses. Put a metal teaspoon in each glass. Carefully pour in the hot coffee and stir to dissolve the sugar.

Stir a tablespoon of whiskey into each glass. Remove the spoon and hold it upside-down over the glass. Slowly pour the cream over the back of the spoon on to the hot coffee so that it floats on the surface. Serve immediately.

# COFFEE ICE CREAM WITH PECANS

*Caramelized pecans make a wonderful contrast in texture and flavour to this fabulous coffee ice cream.*

**Serves 4–6**

*300ml/¹/₂ pint/1¹/₄ cups milk*

*15ml/1 tbsp demerara sugar*

*25g/1oz/3 tbsp finely ground coffee*
   *or 15ml/1 tbsp instant coffee*
   *granules or powder*

*1 egg plus 2 egg yolks*

*300ml/¹/₂ pint/1¹/₄ cups double cream*

*15ml/1 tbsp caster sugar*

**For the pecans**

*115g/4oz/1 cup pecan halves*

*50g/2oz/¹/₄ cup soft dark*
   *brown sugar*

COOK'S TIP

*Remember to transfer the ice cream from the freezer to the fridge 30 minutes before serving. It will then be soft enough to scoop easily.*

Heat the milk and demerara sugar to boiling point. Remove from the heat, sprinkle on the coffee and leave to stand for 2 minutes. Stir well, cover and cool. Place the egg and egg yolks in a heatproof bowl and whisk until thick and pale.

Strain the coffee mixture into a clean pan, heat to boiling point, then pour on to the eggs in a steady stream, beating constantly. Set the bowl over a pan of simmering water and heat gently, stirring all the time, until the mixture thickens. Cool and then chill in the fridge. Whip the cream with the caster sugar until soft peaks form. Fold the cream into the coffee custard and freeze in a covered container. Beat the mixture twice at hourly intervals and then leave to freeze until firm.

To caramelize the nuts: preheat the oven to 180°C/350°F/Gas 4 and spread the nuts in a single layer on a baking sheet. Toast them in the oven for 10–15 minutes until golden. Meanwhile, place the brown sugar in a heavy pan with 30ml/2 tbsp water and heat gently, shaking the pan occasionally, until the sugar dissolves completely and the syrup clears. When the syrup begins to bubble, add the pecans and cook for 1–2 minutes. Spread the nuts on a lightly oiled baking sheet and leave to cool.

Scoop the coffee ice cream on to pretty dishes and serve with a few caramelized pecans.

# Special Occasion Desserts

*If you're looking for something out of the ordinary to end a meal, you can never go wrong with a delicious coffee dessert. Whether starring by itself or blended with chocolate for a dark and luscious mocha taste, these recipes are the perfect, indulgent way to mark a special occasion.*

# MOCHA TRUFFLES WITH TIA MARIA

*These irresistible truffles are perfect for passing around at a dinner party or as a special Christmas treat.*

**Makes about 25**

*175g/6oz dark chocolate, broken*
*into squares*
*50g/2oz/4 tbsp unsalted butter*
*10ml/2 tsp instant coffee granules*
*30ml/2 tbsp double cream*
*225g/8oz/4 cups Madeira cake*
*crumbs*
*50g/2oz/¹/₂ cup ground almonds*
*30ml/2 tbsp Tia Maria or other*
*coffee liqueur*
*cocoa powder, chocolate vermicelli or*
*ground almonds, to coat*

COOK'S TIP
*You can melt chocolate using*
*your microwave. Place the*
*chocolate in a non-metallic bowl*
*with the butter and coffee. Cover*
*with clear film and microwave*
*for 2–3 minutes on Medium.*
*Stir and continue microwaving*
*until the chocolate has melted.*

Place the broken chocolate in a heatproof bowl with the butter and instant coffee. Stand the bowl over a saucepan of simmering water and heat until the chocolate and butter have melted and the coffee has dissolved. (Do not let the water boil or let the bottom of the bowl touch the water, or the chocolate will overheat.)

Remove the bowl from the heat and stir in the cream, cake crumbs, ground almonds and coffee liqueur.

Chill the mixture until firm and then shape into small balls. Roll the balls in cocoa powder, chocolate vermicelli or ground almonds and place in foil petit four cases for serving.

# CHOCOLATE LOAF AND COFFEE SAUCE

*This wonderfully rich, uncooked chocolate cake has the texture and richness of mousse. The cool coffee sauce makes a delicious contrast.*

**Serves 6–8**

*175g/6oz plain chocolate, chopped*

*50g/2oz/4 tbsp butter*

*4 large eggs, separated*

*30ml/2 tbsp rum or brandy*
   *(optional)*

*chocolate curls and chocolate-covered*
   *coffee beans, to decorate*

**For the coffee sauce**

*600ml/1 pint/2½ cups milk*

*4 egg yolks*

*50g/2oz/¼ cup caster sugar*

*5ml/1 tsp vanilla essence*

*15ml/1 tbsp instant coffee granules or*
   *powder, dissolved in 30ml/2 tbsp*
   *hot water*

Line a 1.2 litre/2 pint/5 cup terrine or loaf tin with clear film, smoothing it evenly over the base and sides. Place the chocolate in a heatproof bowl set over a pan of simmering water and stir until melted. Remove the bowl from the heat and beat in the butter and egg yolks, one at a time, and rum or brandy, if using. Whisk the egg whites until fairly stiff. Stir one third of the egg whites into the chocolate mixture and then fold in the remaining whites. Pour into the loaf tin, cover and freeze until ready to serve.

Make the coffee sauce: bring the milk to a simmer over medium heat. In a separate bowl, whisk the egg yolks and sugar for 2–3 minutes until thick and pale then whisk in the hot milk. Return the mixture to the pan and heat gently stirring all the time. When the custard has thickened, strain into a chilled bowl and stir in the vanilla essence and coffee. Set aside to cool, stirring occasionally. Chill.

To serve, dip the base of the loaf tin in hot water for 10 seconds and invert the dessert on to a serving plate. Peel off the clear film. Cut the loaf into slices and serve with the coffee sauce, decorated with chocolate curls and chocolate-covered coffee beans.

# COFFEE AND CHOCOLATE BOMBE

*This is a fantastic Italian dessert – a luxurious combination of coffee and vanilla ice cream, flavoured*
*with chocolate and amaretti biscuits and bound together with Marsala-soaked sponge fingers.*

**Serves 6–8**

*15–18 sponge fingers*

*about 175ml/6fl oz/³⁄4 cup*
  *sweet Marsala*

*75g/3oz amaretti biscuits*

*about 475ml/16fl oz/2 cups coffee ice*
  *cream, softened*

*about 475ml/16fl oz/2 cups vanilla*
  *ice cream, softened*

*50g/2oz plain chocolate, grated*

*chocolate curls and sifted cocoa*
  *powder, to decorate*

### COOK'S TIP

*In Italy, this dessert is called*
*zuccotto from the word zucca,*
*meaning pumpkin. Special*
*pumpkin or dome-shaped*
*moulds are available for making*
*zuccotta, but a pudding basin*
*is the next best thing.*

Line a 1 litre/1³⁄4 pint/4 cup pudding basin with a large piece of damp muslin, letting it hang over the side. Trim the sponge fingers so that they are roughly the same height as the basin. Pour the Marsala into a shallow dish and dip the sponge fingers, one by one, into the Marsala, turning them quickly so that they become saturated but do not disintegrate. Arrange the fingers around the outside of the basin. Fill in the base and any gaps around the side with the trimmings or with other sponge fingers cut to fit. Chill for about 30 minutes.

Crush the amaretti biscuits in a large bowl and add the coffee ice cream and any remaining Marsala. Beat well until mixed and then spoon the mixture into the finger-lined basin. Press the ice cream against the sponge to form an even layer with a hollow in the centre. Freeze for 2 hours.

Place the vanilla ice cream and grated chocolate in a bowl and fold together until evenly mixed. Spoon the mixture into the hollow in the centre of the mould and smooth the top. Cover with the overhanging muslin and freeze overnight.

To serve, run a palette knife between the muslin and the basin and unfold the top of the muslin. Place a chilled serving plate on top of the basin, then invert the two so that the bombe is upside down on the plate. Remove the basin and carefully peel off the muslin. Decorate the bombe with chocolate curls and sifted cocoa powder. Serve at once.

# ICED COFFEE AND NUT MERINGUE

*This frozen dessert is surprisingly easy to make, yet looks impressive and tastes divine.*

**Serves 8–10**

*175g/6oz/1 cup hazelnuts, toasted*

*275g/10oz/1¹/₃ cups caster sugar*

*5 egg whites*

*1 litre/1³/₄ pints/4 cups coffee ice cream, slightly softened*

*white chocolate curls and fresh raspberries, to decorate*

**For the chocolate cream**

*475ml/16fl oz/2 cups whipping cream*

*275g/10oz plain chocolate, melted and cooled*

*30ml/2 tbsp Tia Maria or other coffee liqueur*

---

**COOK'S TIP**

*If you don't intend to serve the meringue immediately, chill in the freezer until the chocolate cream is firm and then wrap in foil or freezer wrap.*

---

Preheat the oven to 160°C/325°F/Gas 3 and line three baking sheets with non-stick baking paper. Mark a 20cm/8in circle on each sheet and turn the paper over. Chop the hazelnuts in a food processor, add a third of the sugar and process again until finely ground.

Whisk the egg whites until they form soft peaks. Gradually add the remaning sugar, 30ml/2 tbsp at a time, whisking all the time until the whites are stiff and glossy. Fold in the nut mixture. Divide the meringue among the baking sheets, spreading the mixture out so that it is just within the marked circles. Bake in the oven for 1 hour until firm and dry. Turn off the oven and allow the meringues to cool, then peel off the paper.

Beat the ice cream until smooth and then spread half over one meringue layer. Top with a second meringue layer and spread with the remaining ice cream. Top with the last meringue layer and press down gently. Wrap and freeze for at least 4 hours until firm.

To make the chocolate cream: beat the whipping cream until soft peaks form and then fold in the cooled melted chocolate and liqueur. Place the meringue cake on a serving plate and spread the chocolate cream over the top and sides of the meringue. Return to the freezer until the chocolate cream is firm. To serve, let the meringue stand for 15 minutes at room temperature to soften slightly before cutting. Serve decorated with white chocolate curls and raspberries.

# MOCHA CREAM CHOCOLATE CUPS

*A glorious mocha-flavoured mascarpone filling is piled into delicate chocolate cups.*

**Serves 6**

*1 egg yolk*

*30ml/2 tbsp caster sugar*

*2.5ml/1/2 tsp vanilla essence*

*250g/9oz/generous 1 cup mascarpone
  cheese*

*120ml/4fl oz/1/2 cup strong
  brewed coffee*

*15ml/1 tbsp cocoa powder*

*30ml/2 tbsp coffee liqueur*

*16 amaretti biscuits*

*cocoa powder, for dusting*

**For the chocolate cups**

*175g/6oz plain chocolate, broken
  into squares*

*25g/1oz/2 tbsp unsalted butter*

COOK'S TIP

*When making the cups, don't
spread the chocolate too evenly.
Aim for fairly uneven edges,
which will give a frilled effect.*

Make the chocolate cups: cut out six 15cm/6in rounds of non-stick baking paper. Melt the chocolate squares with the butter in a heatproof bowl over barely simmering water and stir until smooth. Spread a spoonful of the chocolate mixture over each paper circle to within about 2cm/3/4in of the edge. Carefully lift each paper round and drape it over an upturned teacup or ramekin so that the edges curve over into frills. Leave until completely set and then gently lift off and peel the paper away to reveal the chocolate cups.

Make the filling: beat the egg yolk and sugar in a bowl until smooth and then stir in the vanilla essence and mascarpone cheese. Mix until smooth and creamy. In a separate bowl, mix the coffee, cocoa and liqueur. Break up the biscuits roughly and stir into the coffee mixture.

Place the chocolate cups on individual plates and divide half of the biscuit mixture among them. Spoon over half of the mascarpone mixture and then repeat with a layer of the remaining biscuits, including any remaining liqui. Top with the rest of the mascarpone mixture. Dust with cocoa powder and serve at once.

# MOCHA CREAM POTS

*This classic French dessert is known as* pots de crème. *The addition of coffee gives it an exotic touch.*

**Serves 8**

*15ml/1 tbsp instant coffee granules*
*or powder*
*475ml/16fl oz/2 cups milk*
*75g/3oz/1/3 cup caster sugar*
*225g/8oz plain chocolate, chopped*
*10ml/2 tsp vanilla essence*
*30ml/2 tbsp Tia Maria or other*
*coffee liqueur*
*7 egg yolks*
*whipped cream and cake decorations,*
*to decorate*

Preheat the oven to 160°C/325°F/Gas 3. Place the instant coffee in a saucepan and stir in the milk. Add the sugar and heat until just boiling, stirring constantly until the coffee and sugar have dissolved. Remove the pan from the heat, add the chocolate and stir until the chocolate has melted and the sauce is smooth. Stir in the vanilla essence and coffee liqueur.

In a large bowl, lightly beat the egg yolks and then beat in the chocolate mixture, mixing until well blended. Strain into a large jug and pour into eight ramekin dishes or small ovenproof cups. Place these in a roasting tin and pour enough boiling water into the tin to come halfway up the sides of the ramekins.

Bake in the oven for 30–35 minutes until the custard is just set and a knife inserted into the custard comes out clean. Transfer the dishes to a baking sheet and allow to cool, then cover and chill completely. Decorate with whipped cream and tiny cake decorations and serve.

**COOK'S TIP**

*It is usual to strain the mocha egg mixture to remove any bits of egg white. However, it is not essential and the dessert tastes delicious either way.*

# MOCHA BRAZIL LAYER GATEAU

*This wonderfully rich dessert is a layered gâteau consisting of both sponge cake and meringue discs. The combination of mocha and Brazil nuts is particularly delicious.*

**Serves 12**

**For the meringue**

*3 egg whites*

*115g/4oz/½ cup caster sugar*

*75g/3oz/¾ cup Brazil nuts, toasted and finely ground*

*10ml/2 tsp instant coffee granules, dissolved in 15ml/1 tbsp hot water*

**For the mocha gâteau**

*115g/4oz/⅔ cup plain chocolate chips*

*4 eggs*

*115g/4oz/½ cup caster sugar*

*115g/4oz/1 cup plain flour*

*5ml/1 tsp baking powder*

**For the icing**

*50g/2oz/⅓ cup plain chocolate chips*

*15ml/1 tbsp instant coffee granules or powder, dissolved in 30ml/2 tbsp hot water*

*600ml/1 pint/2½ cups double cream chocolate triangles and chocolate-covered coffee beans, to decorate*

Preheat the oven to 150°C/300°F/Gas 2. Draw two 20cm/8in circles on a sheet of non-stick baking paper and place on a baking sheet. Whisk the egg whites until stiff and then gradually whisk in the sugar, until the mixture is thick and glossy. Fold in the nuts and coffee. Spread the meringue inside the marked circles on the baking sheets and bake in the oven for 1¾–2 hours until golden. Transfer to a wire rack and peel away the baking paper.

Increase the oven temperature to 180°C/350°F/Gas 4 and grease and line a 20cm/8in round springform tin. To make the gâteau: melt the chocolate chips and cool slightly. Whisk together the eggs and sugar until the mixture is very pale and thick. Stir in the melted chocolate. Sift the flour and baking powder together and fold into the whisked mixture. Pour into the prepared tin and bake for 40–45 minutes until firm and springy to the touch. Transfer the cake to a wire rack, peel away the paper and cool completely.

To make the icing, heat the chocolate chips and dissolved coffee in a bowl over a pan of simmering water, stirring until the chocolate has melted. Remove from the heat. Whip the cream until it holds soft peaks and stir into the mocha mixture.

Cut the cake horizontally into three equal layers and assemble the gâteau with a layer of sponge, a little of the icing and a meringue disc, finishing with a layer of the sponge. Reserve a little icing for piping and coat the cake with the rest, making a swirling pattern over the top. Decorate with piped icing, triangles of chocolate and chocolate-covered coffee beans.

# WHITE CAPPUCCINO GATEAU

*An unusual cake flavoured with white chocolate and coffee, coated with a sumptuous white chocolate frosting.*

**Serves 8**

*4 eggs*

*115g/4oz/1/2 cup caster sugar*

*15ml/1 tbsp strong brewed coffee*

*2.5ml/1/2 tsp vanilla essence*

*115g/4oz/1 cup plain flour*

*75g/3oz white chocolate,*
*    coarsely grated*

*white chocolate curls, to decorate*

*cocoa powder or ground cinnamon,*
*    for dusting*

**For the filling**

*120ml/4fl oz/1/2 cup double cream*

*15ml/1 tbsp Tia Maria or other*
*    coffee liqueur*

**For the white chocolate frosting**

*175g/6oz white chocolate*

*75g/3oz/6 tbsp unsalted butter*

*115g/4oz/1 cup icing sugar*

*90ml/6 tbsp double cream*

*15ml/1 tbsp Tia Maria or other*
*  coffee liqueur*

Preheat the oven to 180°C/350°F/Gas 4. Grease two 20cm/8in round sandwich cake tins and line the base of each with non-stick baking paper. Whisk the eggs, caster sugar, coffee and vanilla essence until the mixture is pale and thick. Sift half the flour over the mixture and fold in evenly. Carefully fold in the remaining flour with the grated white chocolate.

Divide the mixture between the prepared tins and smooth the tops. Bake in the oven for 20–25 minutes until firm and golden brown, then turn out on to a wire rack and leave to cool completely.

To make the filling: whip the cream and coffee liqueur in a bowl until the mixture holds soft peaks. Spread over one of the cakes and place the other on top.

To make the white chocolate frosting: melt the chocolate with the butter in a heatproof bowl set over hot water. Remove from the heat and beat in the icing sugar. Whip the cream in a separate bowl until it just holds its shape, then beat into the chocolate mixture. Allow the mixture to cool, stirring occasionally, until it begins to hold its shape.

Stir the coffee liqueur into the frosting. Spread over the top and sides of the cake, swirling with a palette knife. Top with curls of white chocolate and dust with cocoa powder or ground cinnamon.

# INDEX

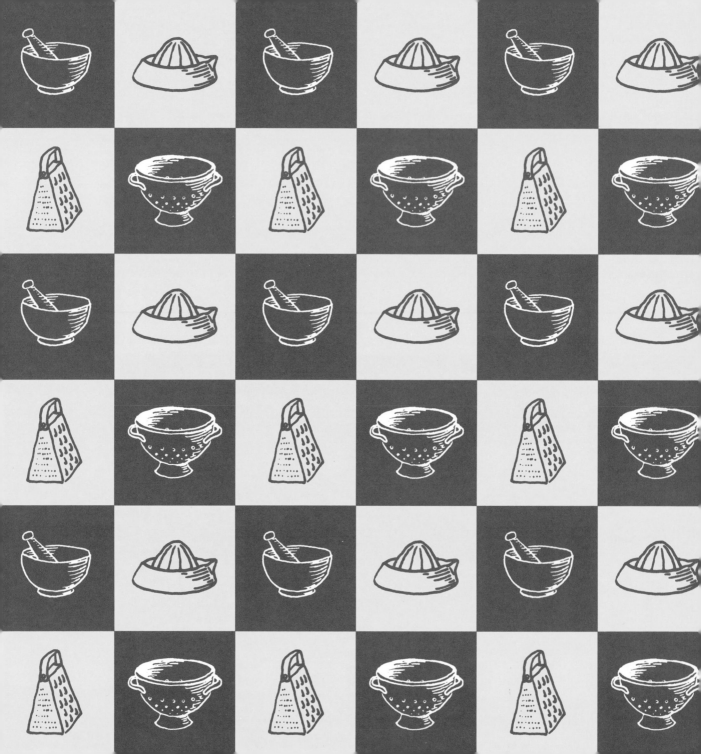